Moscow ●

Baltic Sea

POLAND   Warsaw ●

ague ●

CHOSLOVAKIA

enna ●
STRIA

● Budapest
HUNGARY

Belgrade ●   ROMANIA
YUGOSLAVIA

BLACK   SEA

● BULGARIA

ADRIATIC SEA

ALBANIA

Istanbul ○

Ankara ●

TURKEY

ALY

GREECE

Athens ●

SICILY

○ MALTA

CRETE

CYPRUS ○

SYRIA

NEAN   SEA

Beirut ○   ● Damascus

PALESTINE
Tel Av ●

oli

TRANS-JORDON

○ SUEZ
Cairo ●

I B Y A

EGYPT

CORPORAL HAGGIS

The Wartime Story of a Muscovy Duck
September 1943 - May 1945

CORPORAL HAGGIS

The Wartime Story of a Muscovy Duck
September 1943 - May 1945

Frank and Julian Akers-Douglas

Illustrated by Angelika Elsebach

The Book Guild Ltd
Sussex, England

The Book Guild Ltd
25 High Street
Lewes, Sussex

First published 1996
Frank and Julian Akers-Douglas, 1996
Set in Palatino
Typesetting by Acorn Bookwork, Salisbury

Printed in Great Britain by
Biddles Ltd.
Guildford and Kings Lynn

A catalogue record for this book is available from the British
Library

ISBN 1 85776 053 0

For Daniel, Joseph and Jamie

ACKNOWLEDGEMENT

What we have written down in this book has been very much a family project. From her earliest childhood memories, Julian and her brothers and sister were captivated by their father recounting to them at bedtime the adventures of Haggis. The timeless quality that he brought to the story and the way in which he managed to combine the horror of war with the emotion of a living creature encapsulated all that is essential in entrancing young minds and hearts.

We have tried to be as faithful to the original facts as possible. Whilst some of the details may have been misplaced with the passage of time, all of the episodes described in the following pages are true. We are indebted to John Bruntisfield for his enthusiastic support in providing the original information and then in checking the script and feeding us so much detail to bring it all back to life.

Angelika Elsebach's drawings wonderfully illustrate both Haggis himself and the world he was caught up in at the time. We are deeply grateful to her for so spontaneously joining in the project.

Our thanks also are due to Major J T Morton of the Royal Scots Dragoon Guards and to the Tank Museum, Bovington for their help and advice.

And lastly, of course, there is Smudger himself, who by his adoption of the duck made this really happen.

Frank and Julian Akers-Douglas

PREFACE

Corporal Haggis was a real live Muscovy duck and this is a true story. Doun Tha Whaha and its crew were in Italy in 1943; I believe that the four men in the crew are no longer alive or perhaps, as old soldiers, I should say they have faded away. However, the reality of Corporal Haggis still survives in the memories of the few remaining old soldiers who served with him.

Animals have ever been the companions of fighting men; warfare for centuries could not have been waged without the cooperation of the horse. Who, even today, has ever seen a military event when a dog has not appeared and interrupted the procession? Many of today's regiments and formations retain official mascots which parade with them on public occasions. It is not fanciful to suppose that these official mascots directly descend from soldiers' unofficial pets.

However, so far as experience goes, Haggis is unique. Armies have marched behind eagles and with cockerels at their head. The Royal Navy has, of course, sailed with wrens! Only one tank has ever fought with a duck in its crew. For make no mistake, Corporal Haggis was a very real and very valuable crew member. A warm-blooded, trusting little creature with whom to share fears, fatigues and anxieties – a beating heart, to comfort and to be comforted, filled a need that nothing else could in the subconscience of his human companions and in the cold, comfortless, mechanical environment of an armoured fighting vehicle, a helpless, living creature to be loved and to be cared for was a treasure beyond price.

Here then is the story of Haggis, a Royal Scots Grey, who fought in a tank in Italy, at the invasion of France and through North-West Europe to the Baltic coast, where the British Army met with the Russian Army.

The Lord Bruntisfield, O.B.E., M.C., T.D.

1

Just outside a small town called Wismar on the Baltic coast, a huge oak tree stands fully sixty feet tall, crowned by its vast umbrella of green.

There are two things which are extraordinary about this tree. First, it is ninety-two years old and has survived - virtually unscathed - two violent World Wars. Secondly, it marks the spot where, on a sad day in May 1945, a very special grave was dug. That great old oak tree still stands to the memory of Corporal Haggis.

Haggis was a Muscovy duck.

2

For three long wearying years the war had raged across Africa and Europe and soldiers from a great number of countries had been away from their homes and families.

The Royal Scots Greys – The Greys – had fought their way through the Western Desert in North Africa and had reached Tripoli. Some three months after they had arrived, the order came for them to sail to Italy. They embarked on 4 September 1943.

At the break of day on 9 September 1943, The Greys landed

from the sea on to the beaches near Salerno in a bay south of Naples.

This was not like arriving from a boat for a picnic at the seaside. The enemy was waiting for them and a massive onslaught of shooting started even before the landing-craft had beached. The infantry soldiers had to jump waist-high into the sea and wade ashore through the terrifying cacophony of bullets and explosions. The diesel-engined Sherman tanks, only recently acquired by The Greys with other new vehicles, rolled from the boats and belly-flopped into the shallow Mediterranean water, followed by all the rest of the paraphernalia that an army has to take with it into battle.

The exact spot where they landed was called Spinata, which is at the mouth of a narrow river called the Tusciano. It flows between low hills on to the flatlands above the beaches at Salerno. It was up from these beaches that The Greys headed in their tanks with the vanguard moving forward. They fought fiercely for every inch of ground gained.

The guns and mortars blazed in the morning half-light and the tanks had to break out of their beachhead and move through the contourless land, which was a patchwork of vineyards and apple orchards, with fields of tobacco and of tomatoes reaching to the wooded hills in the distance. This made clear sight ahead difficult and progress was painfully slow. However, the numerous drainage ditches, some half-full of murky water, gave good cover when needed.

The weather conditions were horrendous and it had rained for most of the day. Eight of the cumbersome tanks had become totally unable to move in the sticky mass of mud, and bulldozers, with the help of the men, had had to pull them free whilst the battle raged on all around.

As the day wore on, the fighting began to die down. Word came that the regiment would go no further until the next day and that they should look for secure positions in which to conceal their tanks and themselves overnight. They had also now reached a safe de-waterproofing point – the tanks and other vehicles had had special exhausts fitted to enable them to drive through the water as they landed. These exhausts were knocked off now that there was a lull in the fighting.

3

And so it was, on that battle-torn day in September 1943, that one of The Greys' Sherman tanks took shelter a few hundred yards from the shore in a typical little Italian farmyard. The owners, through fear, had fled some days before as rumours of the Allied landings intensified. There was a group of earth and brick buildings and the roof of one had long since given up the struggle and collapsed. Vigorous creeper had spread the length of a crumbling wall bordering the side of the farmyard, and strewn about the yard were a tatty collection of farm implements, broken and of little use now. The farmhouse itself was bleached by the scorching Mediterranean sun and two of its windows were hanging forlornly on their rusty hinges.

The huge tank moved in and parked between an old, unkempt olive grove and a battle-scarred cowshed. With great relief the crew scrambled slowly out of the turret and jumped down to stretch their legs, dust down their trousers and examine their new surroundings. They were exhilarated but exhausted after the success of the battle up from the beach and above all happy to be free from the cramped conditions of the tank. The commander walked over towards the shed to see whether it would provide suitable sleeping accommodation for the night.

He pushed open the door and tried to adjust his eyes to the darkness inside, making out some bales of musty hay from the

year before and several wooden pallets lying haphazardly around. Three old cartwheels had just come into focus, when there was an almighty commotion and a large Muscovy drake appeared. The commander was startled by the unexpectedly big black, dark-green and white bird flapping alarmingly over towards him from the far end of the barn. In the half-light of the building, the birds's red crown reinforced its anger at the intruder. There was no quacking – just an indignant and persistent whistling, hissing noise.

As the duck scurried to the doorway, the commander shouted to the gunner behind him to grab the duck so that they could at last have a wholesome supper. The gunner lurched at it but to no avail. The bird was far more agile than he had first thought and managed to evade the grasp of the hungry man. The wireless operator, who was close to him, ran after the squawking bird into the farmyard, unbuttoning his shirt as he went. With a

terrific lunge he somehow managed to throw his shirt over the bird and then to spread-eagle himself on top of it. Pinned down in this unceremonious way, it began another series of hissing and blowing noises. Proudly the soldier struggled to his feet with the squirming bundle, a broad grin on his face.

The driver had now come up and was helping to disentangle the bird from the wireless operator's shirt. Feathers flew into the air as it emerged. Gripping it firmly by its wings, they carried it triumphantly back to the tank, excited at the thought of the excellent dinner they were going to have on their first night in Italy.

The duck looked startled. It was as though it knew that it was in dire trouble and gave a frantic squirm. It would have made good its escape had the driver not make a grab for its back leg. This left the Muscovy dangling indelicately upside down, furiously flapping its wings in a vain attempt to get away and noisily complaining at its predicament.

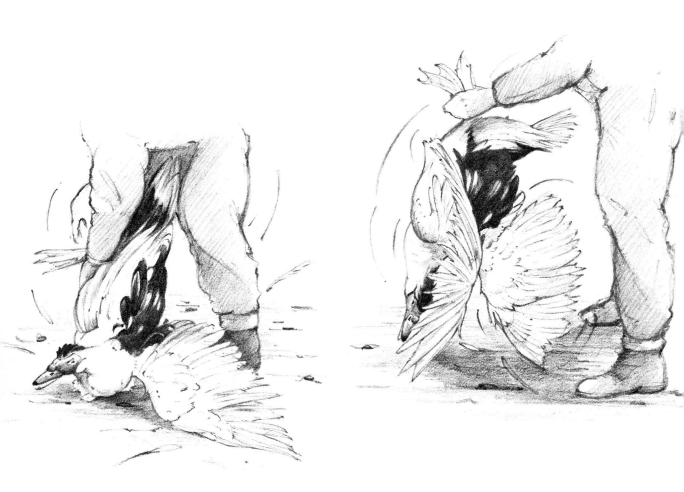

The whole tank crew had by now excitedly gathered around and were on the point of deciding who should wring the poor bird's neck, when the tank's wireless crackled urgently into life. It was an order to move out immediately towards the high hills and face a counter-attack at Battipaglia. This was a small railway town with a large tobacco factory. It lay in flat farm land, surrounded by maize fields, olive trees, tobacco plant-ations and vineyards and overlooked on the landward side by rising hills. There were many dead sheep and cattle in the fields, killed by shell fire in the very heavy fighting. Other dairy cows stood in obvious discomfort through lack of being milked. At once the fun of the farmyard was forgotten as the soldiers scrambled back into the tank, preparing again for battle.

4

The tank was called Doun Tha Whaha, which is Glaswegian slang for an outing down the River Clyde to Rothesay. The crew had chosen this name for their tank because it brought such strong memories of home to them all – in fact the gunner had been working on a Clyde steamer called *The Waverley* before the war had started and had many times been 'down the water'.

As the driver slithered towards the controls at the bottom of the tank, he suddenly realised that he was still clutching the bird, which by now had almost frozen in its fear of what was about to befall it. In all the excitement following the wireless message he had completely forgotten to let go of the crew's supper.

And now it was too late. He stuffed the bird down between his legs, trapping the exhausted creature, and concentrated on manoeuvring the tank towards Battipaglia and the battle.

It turned out to be a very fierce fight, full of horrendous noise and calamity, and it continued on and off throughout the night. Doun Tha Whaha was in the thick of it, crawling over rough ground and firing towards the enemy lines. Each time the gun was fired, the tank would jolt violently and as the breech opened, the shell-case would crash to the floor, startling the petrified duck and surrounding it with a heavy cloud of cordite smoke.

The fighting, if not the battle, ended as dawn broke and a watery sun bathed the countryside. The men were exhausted and thinking only of sleep and rest. Doun Tha Whaha had stopped in a little thicket of cypress trees and an eerie quiet followed the noise and commotion of battle.

As the crew began to relax, what should they see sitting on top of the pile of brass shell-cases in the bottom of the tank but the Muscovy duck preening its feathers and looking for all the world as if he had just woken up in the barn at his farmyard home. As each member of the crew saw the black, green and white creature with his red wattle, they gazed in amazement and knew, of course, that he had become their friend.

The duck knew it too.

5

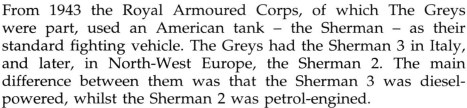

From 1943 the Royal Armoured Corps, of which The Greys were part, used an American tank – the Sherman – as their standard fighting vehicle. The Greys had the Sherman 3 in Italy, and later, in North-West Europe, the Sherman 2. The main difference between them was that the Sherman 3 was diesel-powered, whilst the Sherman 2 was petrol-engined.

Doun Tha Whaha was home to five Scots Greys. There was the commander, the gunner and the wireless operator, who would all be squeezed into the turret, whilst the driver and the lap gunner sat in the hull at the front of the tank, to the left. The driver had clutch and accelerator pedals and two hand levers which were brakes and enabled him to steer the vehicle by braking one track or the other. As the driver only had to hold these levers when actually turning, he was perfectly able to hold on to the duck on his lap.

The commander in the turret gave the driver directions through the intercom. The turret was entirely separate and shaped a bit like a flowerpot, with the bottom extending down into the body of the tank itself. The breech of the gun took up space forward. The gunner sat on the left of it with his head near the armoured front where his periscope was positioned. The wireless operator (who also doubled up as the loader) sat on his right with his wireless behind him. The commander sat

(or sometimes stood) at the rear of the turret, to the left of the breech. When the gun was fired, the breech recoiled a good foot past his right arm as it ejected the brass shell-case. This was a particularly dangerous time for the commander, in the very cramped conditions.

The tank had a 75 mm gun and a Browning machine-gun. The ammunition for the main gun was stored in bins around the sides of the 'flowerpot' turret, along with the belts of machine-gun bullets.

The whole turret traversed round 360 degrees and could be turned either by the commander or the gunner.

The only way in or out was through a round entrance above the commander's head. This had a lid which could be shut tight down and also housed a periscope. Normally this was kept open to allow the commander to see better and to allow quicker escape in an emergency. The driver and lap gunner got in and out of the tank through lids above their seats – these were always closed in action. When open, the driver could swivel his seat up so that he could stick his head out of the tank.

There was no easy way to move between the turret and the hull. Bedding, such personal belongings as they had, food and water were all stored in bins or boxes which were secured as best they could be inside the turret and hull. Otherwise, their things were strapped on the back of the turret or on the engine casing.

When they were in battle, the tank would be 'closed down' – this involved the driver steering by using the periscope whilst the commander would peep out of the top of the turret. They would talk to each other through their microphones and hear what was being said in their headphones. This was not easy as the engine was kept running at all times and the racket was deafening, especially if the gun was being fired at the same time. More often than not, only the commander had any idea of what was going on – the wireless operator could hear the wireless but could see nothing, the gunner could see out of the

peri-scope but could hear nothing, with the rest of the crew just hoping for the best.

In the searing summer sun, the dust and flies were awful. There was no let-up by day or by night as the relentless heat exhausted all members of the crew. In winter, the temperature fell to several degrees below freezing and the mud got everywhere. Whatever the season, the duck was forever preening his feathers, letting the loose ones drift away or fall into the bottom of the tank. Muscovies, like all birds, make enormous efforts to keep their plumage good and clean, whatever the conditions they find themselves in.

And it was in the bottom of the tank that he felt the safest when the soldiers were fighting. Happiness and contentment were found in the dark confines of the massive steel tank, along with the companionship of the driver, who was known by all the crew as Smudger. Smudger's real name was Smith but he well knew the origin of his nickname, coming as it did from blacksmiths' communities where the smith was always known as 'Smudger Smith'. Although all the crew had adopted the duck, to Smudger he had become a special friend.

This was a friendship that grew over the next four months as Doun Tha Whaha and The Greys fought their way up through Italy. From Salerno, they moved past Pompeii to Naples and Aversa and then on to Capua. Crossing the Volturno to Tranzi and then along the Garigliano to Teano, they at last arrived at the foothills of the mountain at Monte Cassino. They could not see the monastery itself, as they were in the middle of a chestnut forest with deep ravines and winding roads.

With no great ceremony, the duck had been christened along the way as Haggis by Smudger and the crew. Despite their somewhat cumbersome appearance Muscovies are strong flyers, and they had to clip his wings to stop him from flapping away. In truth, the more Haggis lived with his friends in Doun Tha Whaha the more protected he felt and the less the risk of him trying to abscond. However, he still whistled and hissed when upset or when he wanted attention. He took very little exercise,

31

preferring to waddle about making himself look terribly busy whenever the tank stopped. As with all Muscovy ducks, food was of extreme importance in Haggis' day and he would keep an ever-watchful eye for any opportunity to find tasty morsels.

When on the move and things were quiet, Haggis would sit on the turret and look around as though he was the commander of the tank.

All this was rather different when the tank was involved in battle. Muscovies have a peculiar characteristic, unique to them, of raising along the top of their head a crest of tufty feathers when startled or fearful. This gives a somewhat comical appearance to the poor, frightened creature. Therefore, despite attempting upmost bravery, at the first sound of gunfire Haggis would scuttle down the turret, slither and flutter between the wireless operator and the gunner and sit on the driver's lap and go to sleep.

At least he pretended to go to sleep.

32

Sometimes he just closed his eyes and hoped that the noise and confusion would soon go away. At others, he would bury his head under his wing and hope for the best. And although the driver only had an extremely small area in which to operate and manoeuvre the heavy tank, he never tried to push Haggis off his lap. Quite simply, he felt protected by the bird.

Not every member of the crew was as bonded to Haggis as Smudger. More than once, when perched on top of the turret, Haggis got in the commander's way as he peered through his binoculars and was very brusquely shoved to one side. This prompted much indignation on Haggis' behalf and he would flap off looking for support from his friend Smudger.

The Greys moved further up this region of Italy, liberating a great number of towns and villages from enemy occupation. They fought through many ancient communes devastated by the heavy shelling which inevitably preceded their arrival. They saw stone bridges snapped in two which had, in their prime, proudly spanned wide rivers. At one point, they passed within a few hundred yards of the spot where Hannibal fought his famous battle at Cannae in 216 BC.

Often Haggis would sit on the turret acknowledging the cheering crowds – old and young alike showered fruit and flowers on the troops as the local people swarmed amongst the tanks. The duck would adopt a pose with his bill stuck high in the air and offer the occasional nod towards a particularly noisy

part of the crowd. The novelty of seeing something so simple after so many months of fear and trauma inevitably meant that Haggis was cheered to the echo and fed bits of bread and vegetable and anything else the enthusiastic onlookers had to hand.

As each day ended, the crew would park the tank in as safe a spot as they could find and get out and sleep under their rough army blankets beneath the gnarled olive trees or in the moon-shadow of the tank itself. Despite some hot days, the nights were very cold and Haggis would waddle over to the driver and scrabble at his head as if asking to be allowed in under the warm blanket. It did not take long for Smudger to learn what this particular antic meant and on most nights they would end up sleeping close together under the same cover, Haggis with his head under his wing but with one beady eye fixed on his companion.

6

In a strange and yet very obvious way, the tank took on the role of home to the crew and to Haggis. When the regiment was stood down, a large part of the day was involved in cleaning Doun Tha Whaha inside and out, servicing the engines and stripping down and reassembling the breech of the turret gun. The crew also had to wash their clothes and would drape them over the tank in the hot sun to dry. More than once, Haggis was caught red-handed pecking at the clean clothes and dragging some sock or shirt through the dust and dirt.

Haggis, too, kept himself well turned out and immaculately preened even though he rarely found fresh water to bathe in. By constant attention to himself, he kept his feathers oily clean and always looked pristine – even at his moult time, when he would ensure that his loose and tired feathers were plucked out as soon as he comfortably could. The crew, understandably, were proud of this magnificent drake.

For day after day and for the following weeks, life took on this pattern for Haggis. He was never restricted in where he was allowed to go except when the tank's turret had to be secured in the middle of a battle. Then he was more than happy to sit quietly in the driver's lap, soaking up the security he felt there.

37

During the day, the crew sat about on ammunition boxes or on top of water cans, exchanging stories, writing home or just silently thinking of where they were and what the next day might hold. Sometimes they were fearful, sometimes thoughtful, quite often light-headedly happy but always ready to move off at a moment's notice. The food was prepared on primus stoves, often using cans made out of old petrol tins. Meals were cooked by the crew of each tank and eaten out of metal mess-tins, held

by a hinged handle which too often for safety would give way at a strategic moment, leaving a soldier's lap full of the dish of the day. Bully beef, tinned sausages, bacon, hard-tack biscuits and canned fruit were the staple diet, supplemented only by an occasional chicken or pig, 'taken' from a farmyard.

Tea was the universal drink and was gulped down out of large enamel mugs – every now and again someone would happen upon some beer or wine left behind as the owners fled ahead of an advancing battle.

39

Haggis would sit with the crew while they cooked and ate their meals alongside the tank, happily gobbling up anything that they let fall from their mess-tins. Mealtimes were Haggis' favourite and he adored every moment of looking plaintively at one of the crew as he munched into a biscuit or bully beef. Haggis knew exactly how to ensure that he received more than his fill of the crew's rations. To drink, he would stick his head into a puddle or waddle into the edge of some pond to scoop up water. His delight of all time, however, was to thrust his beak into an enamel mug full of tea and tinned milk.

At night he would potter along beside his friends to the houses or barns which they used for shelter. The most comfortable spot was usually amongst bales of straw or, if their luck was in, on an old mattress. However, without fail, Haggis would settle down beside Smudger, puffing up his feathers for maximum warmth and companionship. On most nights he would sleep peacefully alongside his devoted friend.

Although the bond between Haggis and Smudger was the closest, all of the crew were endeared to the Muscovy duck, with his funny waddling walk and his inquisitive look. In all the time that Haggis had been with the crew, he had never got lost or separated for any length of time. Once in a while he would wander off to find some farm pond to wash in or to hunt for food in the far reaches of a deserted farmyard. He was so contented with his friends that he did not miss other Muscovy ducks and only rarely was he distracted by one of the female ducks that he came across as they travelled up through Italy.

7

Haggis' first Christmas and Hogmanay with his crew were in 1943. They were spent at a little farm near Tranzi. Typical of many old towns in the region, it had small sturdy houses and narrow shaded streets clustered around the church and town hall in the main square. Centuries ago it had been deliberately built on a hilltop to avoid malaria. One of the crew had found a couple of scrawny chickens in the farmyard. Vehicle cooking had been suspended over this period and the squadron cooks came into their own preparing a very special Christmas lunch. The most popular cook amongst Doun Tha Whaha's crew was the gunner and he had made a Christmas pudding out of some dried prunes, biscuit mix and tinned milk. They all fed well that day, none more so than Haggis. After lunch, leaving the men to talk over old memories and happier times, he wandered away to find his favourite spot to get out of the bitter winter cold – sitting on the flat top of the engine covers behind the turret, where the heat of the engines warmed the armour-plate of the tank. There had been a lull in the fighting for a few days over the Christmas period and this enabled training to be carried out. In addition, leave parties to Naples were organised and some local game-shooting was found.

The crew had promoted Haggis to corporal. He was now

Corporal Haggis and had been awarded, with no great ceremony as was the custom, two medals – the Long Service and Good Conduct Medal and the Italy Star. Smudger had made the two corporal's stripes from a spent brass shell-case and he wore these clipped to his wings. Round his neck, attached to an old black bootlace, he wore the cap-badge of the Royal Scots Greys. This was a silver Napoleonic eagle with 'Waterloo' written underneath.

By now he was recognised by most of the men in the regiment. In fact, Smudger was sure that Haggis recognised his name and would come wandering up to any group of soldiers having a snack and wait patiently with his head cocked on one side for the inevitable titbit. Haggis, now almost two and a half years old, had become a large, mature and handsome Muscovy

43

corporal stripes.

long service and good conduct medal.

lace for securing badge around Haggis neck.

Made from spent brass shell cases.

Italy bar.

Cap badge

drake with a full chest on which his Waterloo eagle would bounce as he waddled along on important parade days. Smudger made certain that his corporal's stripes were as clean as any in the regiment. Corporal Haggis could truly be said to be a Royal Scots Grey.

8

By the beginning of 1944 the Allied armies were well advanced in their plans for the invasion of Normandy. As part of this massive movement of armies, The Greys had to hand over all their tanks and other vehicles to The 50th Royal Tanks and return to Naples. From there, they would set sail for Scotland to start training for the invasion. Strange feelings and uneasy thoughts filled the minds and hearts of the crew and their feathered companion. All were aware that Doun Tha Whaha had become more than just a home to them and equally felt the gravity of what lay ahead. Haggis was passed up to Smudger, who was sitting in the back of a three-ton lorry, leaving behind Doun Tha Whaha and the sanctuary and protection which it had given to them amidst all the noise and clutter of war.

All of the soldiers in this area were billeted either in the outskirts of the city or in Naples itself. From there for a week the men were able to relax a little. Parties went to climb Vesuvius, with its impressive volcanic crater still smoking. Those who managed to reach the top could peer into its mysterious depths. The ancient site of Pompeii, strangely resembling a badly bombed town, was also visited by many men in these relaxing days. Naples was another attraction. Haggis lived with the crew but it was very different to the time he spent with them fighting up from Salerno. Smudger was concerned that Haggis might wander off and be mistaken for a good meal by some group of unknowing soldiers. Therefore he was made to live in a ground-floor room of the requisitioned house and was only allowed into the backyard for, to Haggis, an extraordinarily short time each day.

At the end of the week, it was time to start the journey to Scotland. The regiment, with all their kit, marched briskly down the road and reached the outskirts of Naples in good time. From there they headed to the docks. Haggis was resplendent with his shining plumage, his corporal's stripes and cap-badge gleaming on his chest. Although the crowds were not as large or noisy as they had been in some of the towns and villages that they had liberated, he behaved as though for all the world it was totally laid on for him. What Haggis could not know was that Smudger was as proud of Haggis as Haggis was of the crowd.

The regiment left Naples on 28 January. The crew were embarked on to a troop-ship for the journey to Scotland and the exciting reality of some very overdue leave. The ship they were to travel on was an old passenger vessel from the Dutch East India Company which had ploughed the journey from Holland to Indonesia and was called the *Tegelburg*. Its destination was Glasgow, on the River Clyde. It too, along with those it was carrying, had been pressed into service as part of the war effort and for the next several days was to be the home for a great many men of war returning home. It was hideously overcrowded and was part of a convoy of other merchantmen, escorted by a small aircraft-carrier and three or four destroyers. On board there were the best part of a thousand men, of which The Greys accounted for about four hundred. In her civilian days, the *Tegelburg* would have carried no more than one hundred and fifty passengers.

The ship passed through the Straits of Gibraltar and a week later the coast of Ireland could be seen. Scotland was only a few days on from there.

However, as it would be a long and tedious journey and because the ship was extremely crowded, Smudger decided that Haggis had to be kept in a box for his own safety. He set about making a suitable one with slatted sides and a hinged lid. Haggis watched all this with his usual inquisitiveness, little realising what was in store for him.

Once the box was finished, Smudger gathered up Haggis in his arms, placed him gently into the container; closed the lid and made it secure with a piece of string wound around a nail. And this was how Haggis left his homeland and travelled to Scotland.

It took Haggis a while to realise what had happened. It took less time for him to realise that it had been his so-called friend Smudger who had incarcerated him thus. This made him extremely angry and the angrier he got, the noisier he became. Hissing and whistling came from the inside of the box and there was the most frightful commotion as Corporal – *Corporal* – Haggis protested at the lack of freedom that had been forced on him for the first time in his life. There was to be no respite from it. As the ship was so crowded, which could have led to unforseen disaster, Haggis was seldom allowed out of his "prison". All that Smudger could do was push pieces of food through the slatted sides and fill an old tobacco tin full of fresh water every now and again.

Haggis refused to get used to his cramped conditions and would set off the raucous noise at any opportunity. He particularly enjoyed protesting during the inky-black nights, much to the consternation of the men who were trying hard to sleep nearby.

Worse was to follow.

9

As there were so many soldiers on the troop-ship, there were few places to relax and stretch out. Most of the men on board had to sit on their Mae Wests or huddle under the lifeboats on the slippery deck. This was how Smudger sat, always close to Haggis' crate, trying as best he could to calm the frenzied duck. Despite Smudger's attention to Haggis, the Corporal had been worried that several men had given eager looks in his general direction. He was not quite sure why he was worried but something seemed horribly wrong.

Then one day the inevitable happened. Whilst Smudger was down below having his lunch, one of the soldiers spied Haggis' crate. Walking over towards it, he took off his cap and unbuttoned his tunic, rubbing his hands together in anticipation. Haggis was alarmed and struck up his ritual hissing and squawking. The soldier was certain he had found just what he had been looking for, and glancing around to make sure Smudger was nowhere to be seen, he yawned and, with a deeply contented sigh, sat down right on top of Haggis' box. He thought he had found a very comfortable place to sit and rest.

Corporal Haggis was furious. The soldier's bottom was protruding down between the slats and it took Haggis only a moment to open his bill extremely wide and peck the soldier as hard as he could manage. With a yelp, the soldier jumped up from the crate, clutching his behind, and rushed off cursing and swearing as only a Glaswegian can. Haggis was very pleased with himself and briefly his bad temper left him as he cocked his head on one side to see if the man would dare return.

That one didn't but others less in the know soon learnt better!

The rest of the journey to Scotland was slow and boring. The ship was very uncomfortable for everyone, including Corporal Haggis, and the weather became colder and colder. Occasionally the captain of the escorting destroyer would catch a glimpse of an enemy submarine on the radar and immediately everyone was called up on deck to their boat-stations in case it was hit by a torpedo and they had to abandon ship.

No one ever seemed to remember poor Haggis at times like this and he would wake up with a start, as the depth charges were let off over the side whenever an enemy submarine was spotted on the radar.

10

It took ten days to reach Scotland – ten days of heightening excitement at the prospects of a homecoming which dulled the frayed tempers and sharp words that the severely cramped quarters provoked. Haggis was no exception in these trying conditions and as days ran into nights and back into days again, he lost all track of time. The slightest upset caused bad-tempered and noisy reactions by him.

In the dank and grey mid-morning of 7 February 1944, the *Tegelburg* pushed its way up the River Clyde on the last leg of the journey from Italy. It would be another twenty-four hours until the ship was finally allowed to complete its journey past Greenock and Dunbarton to Shieldhall Dock. Haggis, peering between the slats of his crate, could see lots of khaki leggings and heavy black boots clumping past him. This was the soldiers, amidst a lot of commotion and high spirit, gathering up their possessions in readiness for the docking of the *Tegelburg* in Glasgow.

In the distance came the noise of cheering crowds and the approaching boom of a military band. As the ship slid through the oily water towards the dock, a throng of excited people could be seen lining the harbour walls. Rousing music was now filling the air.

Amidst all the excitement of at last getting home to Scotland, word was also spreading amongst the men that the Customs officers intended to search them thoroughly on disembarkation. Even in wartime, alcohol, cigarettes, soap and other luxuries were very strictly rationed and – most severely enforced – no animals or birds at all were to be allowed to be brought ashore off the ship because of the scare of rabies.

And Corporal Haggis was not the only addition to the regiment that had been picked up on The Greys' travels. There were several scruffy little mongrels that had been adopted as close companions by the soldiers, and at least one white rabbit who, like Haggis, had managed to escape the pot when first discovered in southern Italy.

11

As the ship nosed its way towards its jetty, the soldiers hatched a plan to escape the Customs men's methodical search for their pets.

The ship tied up and two huge gangplanks were put to its side. The men bustled and jostled good-humouredly to have the chance to set foot on their native soil again. However, one of the first to reach the quayside had more important thoughts on his mind. He saw in a flash what he needed – an old tom-cat rootling about amongst some reeking dustbins. He picked it up and held it high above his head and started to shout at the top of his voice in a broad Glaswegian accent:

'Come ben! Come ben! Come ben!'

Then he dropped the cat and it shot off in terror across the dockyard. This was the sign the soldiers still on board the *Tegelburg* had been waiting for.

Immediately, they released their dogs – who had seen with great excitement the cat running off across the dockyard – down the gangplank. They were in a high state of anticipation and nothing, let alone Customs officers, could have stopped the flight of mongrels down the two gangplanks in hot pursuit of the startled cat. Needless to say, the cat had made a very good escape but this did not prevent the dogs tearing around the dockyard feverishly running here, there and everywhere as frustrated Customs officers tried in vain to stop them from coming ashore.

Whilst all this was going on, the train to take the regiment to the south coast of England had arrived at the quayside. All of the soldiers disembarked from the ship and boarded it. Those who had had dogs on board took the seats nearest to the doors. Just as the engine was about to move off, each of them stuck their index and middle fingers in their mouth and whistled their pet's call-sign. Immediately, each of the dogs ran straight towards the appropriate carriage, jumped on board and could be seen sitting on their owner's lap as the train chuffed out of Glasgow Docks.

Not one of the dogs had been caught by the Customs officers.

12

Corporal Haggis came ashore very differently.

Each morning on the trip, Haggis ate a breakfast of porridge with Smudger and the crew. It had become something of a ritual and Haggis used to look forward to it expectantly, both for the food but also because it meant that he escaped from his 'prison' for a few brief moments.

On the morning that the ship finally reached Glasgow, Smudger managed to lay his hands on some whisky. He soaked several slices of bread with the strong alcohol and mixed it into Haggis' porridge. Haggis tucked in to it all with great enthusiasm and soon had finished this potent dish. Almost immediately he passed into drunken oblivion.

The unconscious duck was then hidden in the very middle of Smudger's bedroll, which was folded up and strapped on to the soldier's back.

Unfortunately, the episode with the dogs meant that it had taken longer than Smudger had anticipated for him to be able to disembark, given that this particular 'military' exercise did not run as smoothly as might have been hoped. By the time

that it was Smudger's turn to walk off down the gangplank, Haggis had started to come round and was beginning to wriggle and squirm, making increasingly loud protesting noises at the realisation that he was entombed deep inside the scratchy (and by now, hot) bedroll. Sensing the danger to their friend, the rest of the crew immediately started to sing and shout, making as much noise as possible as they walked off down the gangplank, to disguise the duck's distress from the Customs men. Smudger felt Haggis' squirming intensify and he was certain that at any moment he would hear the dreaded shout from one of the stern-faced Customs officers. If it came to it, he was weighing up the chance of making a run for it but, whistling a cheery tune and giving the official a broad smile, he took the final few purposeful strides towards the bottom of the gangplank. Haggis had made his arrival in Scotland undetected.

Eventually he was released from his uncomfortable hiding-place as the train moved off out of Glasgow. He was far from amused at what he had been put through and took some time to be convinced that Smudger could still be trusted.

13

There were no civilians on this train – only soldiers able, almost for the first time in four years, to relax and be away from the constant fear and noise of the front line. Corporal Haggis soon forgot his bad temper at the undignified way that he had been brought ashore. He settled happily enough into a routine of being pampered by the men in the carriage with him.

There was no food carried on the train itself. Instead the train would stop every two or three hours at selected stations where long trestle-tables running the length of the platform were laid out. The soldiers would queue up for bowls of hot stew, sandwiches and mugs of steaming, sweet tea. Cigarettes and chocolate were handed out to all and sundry by the women of the Women's Royal Auxiliary Corps and the Women's Voluntary Service.

Haggis would queue up in front of Smudger and patiently waddle forward on the end of a makeshift lead until he got to the top of the line. There was a major problem, however. As he was way below the table level, none of the WRACs saw Haggis when at last, after what seemed like a never-ending wait, he arrived at the counter. Haggis did not think much of being completely ignored when he got within reach of food. Everyone else was given things to eat and drink and Haggis got nothing for himself. His trick was to let out an extremely long and loud series of hisses and whistles, flapping his wings as well to attract attention. The women were totally taken aback by this strange racket and could not imagine what on earth could be making such a din. When the WRACs saw what it was making all the noise, they fell about with laughter. They fed him chunks of bread soaked in the gravy from the stew.

The train journey eventually came to an end just after midnight on 10 February in Worthing, a town in Sussex on the south coast of England, not more than 50 miles from France. Here The Greys and other regiments were to be involved in preparations for the invasion of France. This entailed both being totally re-supplied with tanks, armoured vehicles and weapons and training on the army ranges to get used to their new equipment. Again, Haggis found himself in the hurly-burly of army life, with so much activity going on but with a correspondingly little amount of attention for him.

However, Smudger – who had been in foreign countries with the rest of the regiment for over four years without a break – was given the longed-for assurance of a month's leave. So within a week of arriving in the South, he and Corporal Haggis were on their way back to Glasgow by train. This time Haggis was in a considerably better mood as he was allowed to wander about the train in comparative freedom on the end of a piece of string. This caused many raised eyebrows as this was a civilian train and Smudger spent much of the journey explaining to people the incredible story of how it was that he had a Muscovy duck as a friend.

14

During March 1944, Smudger had been recalled to Worthing to complete his training. Haggis came too.

The soldiers had no idea of the reason for the training but there was a hive of activity, involving tank manoeuvres, troop movements and incessant loading and unloading from landing-craft. It was not long before most people had a pretty shrewd idea of what they were being prepared for.

In the next three months, the regiment lived in requisitioned houses and spent the days going over battle plans, having equipment issued and generally being kept totally occupied with the preparations. Although Haggis was allowed to stay with the regiment, and in particular with the tank crew, throughout this period, it was a time for soldiers rather than ducks and there were moments when Haggis very definitely felt unloved and ignored.

Unknown to the men, the day drew nearer when they would have to cross the Channel at the start of the invasion. The date had been set by the army commanders for 5 June 1944. At the last moment, the weather conditions and forecast were so bad that the launch of this huge military exercise was postponed for 24 hours. It was this that the last hectic months had been for and those of the men who had guessed at the purpose were relieved at last to be having the training put into practice.

The Greys had marched 80 miles down the coast to Gosport to sail for France. Smudger and the crew crossed in a special ship called a tank landing-craft, which rolled and pitched in the rough seas. They left in the very early hours of 7 June and reached the Normandy beaches in the evening of the same day – the weather was surprisingly calm and sunlit after the difficulties of the crossing, when most of the men had been sea-sick. Haggis had been stowed in the bottom of the craft along with the crew, a frightened bird surrounded by his companions.

They landed on the beaches at a place called Courseulles, which was west of the ancient fishing port of Honfleur. The ramp at the front of the tank landing-craft was lowered and the ship was run up on to the beach. The crew and Haggis were

greatly relieved that there was no fighting as they landed and they were able to disembark their equipment quickly but safely, despite the thick crust of defences that had been thrown up to try and prevent landings.

However, as Haggis accompanied his driver in the tank through France in the days after they landed, they were involved in some very heavy fighting indeed. They made steady but often very slow and dangerous progress. The tanks would hide in shallow dips in the ground which provided some cover in what was otherwise a flat and desolate landscape. They moved through the countryside in formations of three tanks – one going forward to spy out the land and then radioing the two flanking tanks to join it. In a funny way, this movement

resembled a duck's footprint. In the weeks immediately following the invasion, The Greys pressed on through Caen, Villers Bocage, Falaise and to the Somme, but it was at Caen that the worst of the fighting occurred. When the town did eventually fall to the Allies it had been all but destroyed and there had been heavy casualties suffered by both sides. From there they went on to Belgium and Holland, being able to move at much greater speed than hitherto due to the weaker resistance being shown.

There was little for Haggis to do other than to keep himself

as secure as possible in the belly of the tank, and this invariably meant getting as close as he could to the driver and whenever possible nestling securely in his lap. Often he got in the way as Smudger tried to steer the tank in battle or through war-damaged countryside. He had forgotten how the awful noise of battle had so scared him, so long ago now were those days in Italy.

On formal occasions, Haggis would be dressed up with his cap and rank badges. At other times, members of the crew would stroke and caress Haggis in their strong arms and he loved this attention. Little did he realise how important he had become to the crew.

15

They spent the winter months of 1944 and early 1945 living in a variety of village and farm houses in Belgium and Holland.

Christmas was hardly a time of great celebration but Smudger and the others made the best they could of it. They had stopped at Weert, and on Christmas Day itself the soldiers did all they could to make a merry time. The tank had arrived with an old, battered upright piano strapped to it – this had been picked up a few days earlier from a ruined house in a town they had passed through – and a clutch of chickens in a makeshift crate was also tied to the back of the turret.

After they had eaten an excellent Christmas lunch of chicken, potatoes and beans and while they all relaxed, one of the crew played Christmas carols, regimental songs and some distinctly bawdy ballads on the piano, picking out the keys as melodiously as possible. Haggis thoroughly enjoyed himself and made the most of this by sitting on top of the piano. The day was one of those strange events where people forget the awful surroundings they are in and live as if in a sort of fantasy world. For Haggis, that Christmas Day ended with him fast asleep on Smudger's lap.

During the rest of the winter
it was bitterly cold. So cold, indeed, that
on many nights the crews had to move their tanks
every few hours to ensure that they did not freeze into the
mud. Sleeping was not easy and the men would try to get as
much rest as possible either in abandoned houses, old barns or
in cowsheds. Wherever Smudger found himself at the end of
each day, there too would be Haggis loyally sleeping alongside
him.

When time allowed, the crew skated in their heavy army boots on the frozen water of the canals. Smudger would takes Haggis along with him and the duck would half-waddle and half-slide down the icy bank to the canal and slither about in a rather ungainly fashion on the ice. More often than not, this Italian skating duck would end up ignominiously slipping along on his rear with his little legs flapping wildly in the air, making the inevitable hissing noises.
It was fun and light relief from the horrors of war.

They stayed in this area until the middle of February, when they moved to Tilburg before advancing to between the Maas and the Rhine. Here they would meet up with part of the Canadian Army. As ever, Haggis was always at hand, keeping himself out of harm's way but giving confidence and amusing the crew as they completed several difficult actions around the town of Uden.

16

The regiment had to stay in Holland whilst plans were completed for them to cross the Rhine. Eventually they crossed that great river near Xanten on 27 March, using floating bridges that had been laid across it. By the second week in April Haggis and the crew had battled to within a close distance of the River Aller. They fought to cross the river at Rethem and then moved on to take Bremen. They stayed at Bremen until 28 April in countryside that was well-wooded with conifers and where the sandy-soiled plains were divided by tall hedges. Buildings were sparse and flimsily built and posed little problem for the advancing soldiers. More difficulty was encountered from the criss-cross of streams and boggy ground.

On 2 May they finally met up with the Russians (who had been fighting their way from the other direction) on the Baltic coast at Wismar. Miraculously, neither the driver nor the duck had been even slightly hurt through the whole campaign since the invasion.

In addition to The Greys, the Canadian Parachute Regiment had also arrived at Wismar. Everyone knew that the end of the war was very close and the scenes on every road and track told of the imminent finale. The crew and Haggis passed thousands of exhausted men trudging wearily in one direction as they continued their advance in the other.

At one minute past midnight on 8 May 1945, the war was officially declared at an end.

Three days later on 11 May a tremendous victory parade took place in Wismar. Long columns of men and tanks drove triumphantly past the commanding officer of the Allied forces. The occasion was full of ceremony and celebration. As Smudger's tank trundled past generals and other senior officers on the saluting base, there was Corporal Haggis perched on the top of his tank, proudly displaying his cap and rank badges, feeling every bit the conquering hero alongside his comrades.

That night Haggis slept very close to Smudger. By now both the bird and the soldier felt entirely secure and at peace in each other's company. A deep bond had grown between them during their extraordinary wartime journey.

17

A few days later a group of the Canadian gunners were sitting beside their now quietened 25-pounder gun, relaxing in the warm Baltic spring sunshine.

Through a gap in the hedge just to the right of them waddled Corporal Haggis, off duty and not wearing his cap-badge or corporal's stripes. He was on one of his regular hunts for food and attention but had wandered a little further than usual.

He made his way expectantly up to the group of men, eagerly anticipating the usual friendly greeting and a titbit to eat. He cocked his head on one side and sidled closer.

None of the Canadians knew of Corporal Haggis. They had only been in Wismar for a few days and, amidst all the chaos of the end of the war, had not had an opportunity to meet others and swap experiences from the war. They assumed he was just another ordinary Muscovy duck from the local farm. One of them grabbed hold of him by his wing and one of his legs and struck him over the back of his head with his pistol.

Excited at the prospect of a good meal in store, the soldier was on the point of preparing Haggis for the pot when Smudger came through the hedge, calling and looking for his friend.

Hoping and expecting to hear the familiar hissing, whistling noises that told him all was well, Smudger was surprised not only to hear nothing but also to see an excited huddle of Canadian soldiers. He pushed his way through to the middle of the group to see what was happening. Even as he moved forward, a strange sense of dread engulfed him.

In his heart he knew what he was going to find, and as the men parted to let him through, he saw his friend with whom he had shared so much lying there, quite dead.

18

The Corporal was buried with full military honours, beside a young oak tree just outside Wismar. His grave was marked with a little metal plaque, made from the top of an ammunition box.

A DUCK
served as
Acting unpaid Corporal Haggis
A Scots Grey
of the
1939/45 War

Shortly afterwards Smudger and the crew left Wismar. Part of all of them, though, remained for ever at that oak tree.